Amazon Fire TV User Guide

by Tom Edwards and Jenna Edwards

AMAZON FIRE TV USER GUIDE

NEWBIE TO EXPERT IN 1 HOUR!

BY TOM EDWARDS & JENNA EDWARDS

Other Books By Tom & Jenna Edwards

*250+ Best Kindle Fire HDX and HD Apps for the
New Kindle Fire Owner*

Kindle Fire HDX User Guide — Newbie to Expert in 2 Hours!

*All New 7" Kindle Fire HD User Guide —
Newbie to Expert in 2 Hours!*

Chromecast User Guide — Newbie to Expert in 1 Hour!

Apple TV User Guide — Newbie to Expert in 1 Hour!

CONTENTS

A REMINDER ABOUT UPDATES

Before we start, we just want to remind you about the FREE updates for this book. The Amazon Fire TV and indeed all media streaming services, like Apple TV, Roku and the Chromecast, are still in their infancy. The landscape is changing all the time with new services, apps and media suppliers appearing daily.

Staying on top of new developments is our job and if you sign up to our free monthly newsletter we will keep you abreast of news, tips and tricks for all your streaming media equipment.

If you want to take advantage of this, sign up for the updates HERE…

www.Lyntons.com/updates

Don't worry; we hate spam as much as you do so we will never share your details with anyone.

INTRODUCTION

WELCOME

Welcome and thank you for buying the **Amazon Fire TV User Guide: Newbie to Expert in 1 Hour!**, a comprehensive introduction and companion guide to the exciting possibilities that the Amazon Fire TV Media Player has to offer for those new to streaming media to an HDTV.

DO YOU NEED THIS BOOK?

We want to be clear from the very start – if you currently own another media streaming device or consider yourself tech savvy, e.g. the kind of electronics user that intuitively knows their way around any new device or is happy Googling for answers, **then you probably don't need this book**.

We are comfortable admitting that you can probably find most of the information in this book somewhere on Amazon's help pages or on the Internet – if you are willing to spend the time to find it!

And that's the point… this book is a time saving manual primarily written for those new to streaming media devices like Apple TV, Roku TV, Chromecast and the all new Amazon Fire TV.

If you were surprised or dismayed to find how little information comes in the box with your Fire TV and prefer to have to hand, like so many users, a comprehensive, straightforward, step by step guide to finding your way around your new device, **then this book is for you**.

Furthermore the Amazon Fire TV is a brand new piece of kit and there will be new features, channels and games, not to mention tips and tricks, appearing constantly over the coming months. We will be updating this book as these developments unfold, making it an invaluable resource for even the tech savvy.

Even if you are buying the first edition of this book, never fear, you too can keep up to speed with all the new developments by signing up to our free email updates so you'll never miss a thing **www.lyntons.com/updates**.

HOW TO USE THIS BOOK

Feel free to dip in and out of different chapters, but we would suggest reading the whole book from start to finish to get a clear overview of all the information contained. We have purposely kept this book short, sweet and to the point so that you can consume it in an hour and get straight on with enjoying your Amazon Fire TV.

The book aims to answer any questions you might have regarding your Fire TV device such as:

- What is the Fire TV?

- How does the Fire TV work?

- What does the Fire TV do?

- How to setup my Fire TV?

- How to use my Fire TV?

- What can I do with Amazon Fire TV? More than you would have thought!

- What can you stream with the Fire TV?

- How to set up Kindle for Chromecast?

- What are Fire TV's capabilities?

This new Amazon streaming device may be tiny in size, but has huge capabilities. It is a genuine competitor for the likes of Roku, Apple TV, and Chromecast. This book will also look closely at:

- Fire TV apps.

- Using Fire TV settings to get the best out of the device.

- Fire TV troubleshooting.

- Plus much, much more…

As we will be updating this book on a regular basis we would love to get your feedback, so if there is a feature that you find confusing or something else that you feel we've missed then please let us know by emailing us at **ReachMe@Lyntons.com**. Thank you!

So without further ado let's begin…

1. WHAT IS AMAZON FIRE TV?

The fusion of the Internet with the television set has been talked about since the late 1990s, but it only became a reality after the legally-required switch to digital TV starting in 2009.

With the changeover to digital now complete in the United States, the streaming of digital media over the Internet to your TV has finally arrived in force, with a blizzard of new products and services entering the market every month.

When Amazon.com introduced its Fire TV on April 2, 2014, the online retail and digital media giant became the life of the digital party overnight.

The Fire TV is a small, sleek black box that connects to the HDMI port on your HDTV and comes with its own voice-activated remote. After a brief setup sequence to connect the box with your home Internet, you'll have a massive selection of movies, TV shows, music, and gaming at your command on your TV screen.

Although rumors had been circulating for a few years that Amazon was developing a streaming media device, the actual release caught most people by surprise. The surprise has turned out to be a happy one, though, as the Fire TV is easy to set up and even easier to use.

It also gives you access to an amazing amount of programming, both through Amazon's online store and through its partnerships with the big on-demand media companies like Netflix, Hulu Plus, ESPN, and many more.

AMAZON FIRE TV'S COMPETITIVE EDGE

The digital media player market was already very competitive before Amazon joined the pack and upped the ante. According to the publicity surrounding the Fire TV's launch, Amazon used its position as the number one online retailer to tap into customer comments about other set-top boxes like Roku and Apple TV, along with wireless dongles like the Chromecast.

Amazon then used this information to develop the Fire TV and make it do things the others don't. And indeed the Fire TV has some unique features that you can't get on other set-top boxes in the same $99 price range.

Let's take a look…

"Easy" is the theme of Amazon's advertising for the Fire TV: easy to set up, easy to use, easy to search for the shows you want to see. Currently it's the only digital media device with a voice-activated remote (although the competition is no doubt already busy at the drawing board so they can catch up). You simply speak a keyword, such as a movie title or actor, into the remote's built-in microphone, and you'll see the search results on your TV screen so you can select the title you want.

How does it work? Pretty darn well in our experience! Amazon has a very robust search engine, and the remote simply adds voice recognition over the top of it.

For example, if you say "Sharon Stone" into the remote's mic, you'll see all of her films pop up on the Home screen. It sure beats looking them up on a computer, or keying them into an on-screen keyboard one keystroke at a time.

Another big selling point for the Fire TV is that it plugs you into Amazon's gigantic media store, with over 200,000 movies and TV episodes for sale or rental, along with millions of songs you can buy.

It's true that Apple's iTunes store has more movie titles and songs than Amazon, but Amazon has a hook that the other boxes don't have: 40,000 movie titles in the Prime Instant Video library that you can watch for free with a $99 yearly Prime membership.

As for streaming content from the big media companies, the Fire TV currently has just over 20 channels, but Amazon is aggressively pursuing agreements with more streaming media providers, and it has the necessary clout to cut deals with the big names.

Of course nobody can match Roku's selection of 1,200 channels that is similar to a cable TV service, with content ranging from expensive premium subscription bundles to throwaway shopping channels. Apple TV has 30 channels, and Chromecast offers 16 channels. Keep in mind that not all of these channels are free – you pay a monthly subscription fee for the best ones.

Other than Roku, there's not a significant difference among the devices in terms of numbers – you just need to make sure the device you choose has the content you like to watch!

Amazon has also developed its exclusive Advance Streaming and Prediction (ASAP) technology to address a common customer complaint about Internet video streaming: buffering. You've probably experienced stuttering, "hanging", and audio out of sync with the video when you play videos through your computer's web browser, and possibly with other digital media players you've tried out.

Buffering occurs because most people's broadband service isn't up to the heavy bandwidth usage demands of digital media streaming. Amazon's solution is to tap into your user history and use it to predict which movies and TV episodes you might want to watch.

These titles are pre-loaded into your account on their server. If you buy or rent one of these titles, they're already buffered for you and waiting for instant playback A-S-A-P.

As the name implies, the Fire TV is built to pair with Amazon's wildly popular Kindle Fire HDX tablet, which can wirelessly mirror the image on your Kindle screen directly to your HDTV through the Fire TV box.

That includes apps and content available on Kindle but not available through the Fire TV, so if you already own the Kindle HDX, the Fire TV becomes an even more attractive option for media streaming. It's true that the Kindle HDX also mirrors directly to devices like the Samsung Smart TV, but we think the Fire TV is much easier to use – with the Kindle or without it.

Finally, it's obvious that Amazon took a look at its competition and decided to build in something nobody else had: gaming support. The Fire TV box contains a powerful hardware package that's suited for gaming, along with Dolby digital sound.

Even if you're not a gamer, you'll like the smooth, fast loading times it provides. Amazon has also built an external gaming controller unit for the Fire TV, which shows they're serious about developing it as a gaming device.

Currently, there are just over 100 games available for the Fire TV, from bestsellers like Minecraft-Pocket Edition, to unknowns from Amazon's in-house game development studio. Amazon says that thousands of games are on their way to the Fire TV.

While the device can't match the horsepower of the dedicated gaming units like the Playstation or Xbox, there's a sizable difference in the price tag, especially when you figure in all the other things the Fire TV can do.

FIRE TV BY THE NUMBERS

If you'd rather just watch a movie than look at numbers, you can skip ahead to the next section. However, if you're technically inclined, you'll be impressed with the things Amazon has done with the Fire TV.

We can start with its quad-core processor with three times the processing power of the Roku 3 and Apple TV. In addition, the Fire TV has 2 GB of built-in memory – four times as much as the competition.

Internal storage is 8 GB for downloading, saving, and storing content locally, along with free cloud storage for all of your content purchased from Amazon.

The Fire TV's Wi-Fi receiver is dual-band/dual antenna using multiple-input/multiple-output (MIMO) for faster reception. It features Dolby digital sound output and has an optional optical audio output port for 5.1 surround sound audio on high-end home theater systems. Video quality goes up to HD-quality 1080 pixels.

The Fire TV box measures 4.5" x 4.5" x 0.7" and weighs 9.9 ounces. It comes bundled with a power adapter and a voice-activated remote plus two AAA batteries to power it.

The remote is Bluetooth compatible with no line of sight required. An HDMI cable is required but is not included, so you'll have to order your own.

Amazon's Mojito version 3.0 operating system, the same one used for all Kindle Fire HD tablets, powers the Fire TV. Mojito is an Android-based OS built on a forked version of 4.2.2 Jelly Bean.

Now that you know what the Fire TV is, let's look at what you can do with it...

2. WHAT YOU CAN WATCH ON THE FIRE TV

Amazon has entered the digital media market as a power player, thanks to the huge array of movies, TV shows, music, and games available for the Fire TV. Like Apple TV and Chromecast, the Fire TV gives you two ways to access content: either via purchase/rental à la carte, or by subscription.

With à la carte, you buy or rent one title at a time from Amazon's digital media store and play it on your Fire TV or other Internet-connected device.

With a subscription, you download and run an app for one or more of the media channels in the Fire TV line-up and get unlimited access to that channel's entire content library. If you're like most users, you'll end up with a combination of both.

IT'S HARD TO SAY NO TO AMAZON PRIME

From the very first time you set up your Fire TV, Amazon uses it to advertise its Amazon Prime membership service. For a $99 per year subscription fee, Prime offers you 40,000 video titles from the Amazon Instant Video store to stream through your Fire TV and other Internet-connected devices *for free*.

Prime also gives you free two-day shipping on all eligible merchandise orders from the Amazon store totaling $35 or more, and access to the Kindle Owners Lending Library where you can lend and borrow books with other Kindle owners.

You also get one free e-book a month from the Kindle First editor's pick of new releases. If you're a student, the Prime annual fee is reduced to $49 until you graduate.

You get the idea: Amazon offers you lots of nice freebies in hopes that you'll buy more stuff from them. If you're planning to buy or rent videos à la carte from Amazon's store, a Prime subscription looks like a pretty good deal – especially if you also buy a lot of merchandise from them, or if you own a Kindle.

A CLOSER LOOK AT CHANNEL SUBSCRIPTIONS

If you're looking at channel subscriptions, keep in mind that all of the Fire TV's channels require you to download that channel's app from the Amazon app store. An app is simply a piece of software with a specific purpose (for example, the Netflix app's purpose is to display Netflix content).

Many apps for streaming media subscriptions like Netflix and Hulu Plus are free, but for some of them you need to pay a monthly fee to get access through the app to the shows and music you want. All apps can be downloaded directly through your Fire TV, the links we include below are just for your convenience should you wish to check them out on your tablet or computer first. (We explain more about channel subscriptions in **Chapter 4**).

Here's what's currently available for the Amazon Fire TV...

This list is getting longer literally by the day, so keep an eye open for updates. (Please note we don't receive any monetary compensation from the companies we describe below.)

MOVIES AND TV

Movie and TV channels abound on the Fire TV...

Amazon Instant Video: Although Amazon lists it as a "channel" in its line-up, this is simply its "à la carte" video store, similar to Apple TV's iTunes, or the Google Play Movies and Music store for the Chromecast.

Both purchases and rentals are available, and you don't need to be a member of Amazon Prime to use it. No app is required, and there's no monthly subscription fee – you simply choose the title you want, pay, and watch.

Amazon Prime Instant Video: Among the many benefits of buying a $99 annual Amazon Prime membership, you get a subscription to unlimited free streaming from their 40,000 title movie library. No app required, since the Fire TV is tied directly into Amazon's digital store.

Netflix: The giant of digital media streaming. For $7.99 a month, you get unlimited access to their huge selection of movies, TV shows, and original Netflix programming, ad-free. Netflix recently announced that it will increase its monthly subscription rate by $1 or $2 before July 2014 for new customers only, so if you're debating whether to subscribe, grab it now to lock in the low price. The first month is free and you can always cancel.

Hulu Plus: The selection of TV episodes in this upgrade to the free Hulu service is unbeatable. You'll pay a small monthly subscription fee and on top of the great content you get a more limited number of ads than on the free service. The first week is free to try.

Showtime Anytime: Watch movies, sports, comedy, and Showtime original programming. A paid Showtime subscription through your cable or satellite dish plan is required, but Showtime Anytime is a free add-on to your subscription.

Crackle: Like Netflix and Showtime Anytime, Crackle offers movies, TV shows, and original programming. Sony Pictures Entertainment owns Crackle (formerly known as Grouper), so the emphasis is on Sony-produced media. The service is free and has commercials.

YouTube: The Internet's largest library of free videos, featuring movie clips, music, and independently produced original programming.

Huge selection, ad-supported.

Vimeo: This YouTube alternative is a video sharing site that's free to watch, but unlike YouTube, it recently started charging users a $9.95 monthly subscription fee for uploading their videos and an ad-free viewing experience.

Huffpost Live: The Internet streaming version of the left-leaning Huffington Post news and politics website features original programming and live interviews in addition to syndicated videos. The basic version is free and ad-supported.

AOL On: A free, ad-supported news and entertainment video channel from the media giant. AOL On is developing original content and paying its content producers, so watch for changes in the near future.

Flixster: This free social networking channel lets users share movie trailers and reviews of their favorite movies. Flixster is the parent channel of the well known movie review site Rotten Tomatoes and the app includes access to both.

For business programming, take a look at these channels...

Bloomberg TV: This old standby in the business media world features both paid ad-free programming and free ad-supported video content, along with its well-known moving stock ticker.

TastyTrade: This financial trading channel blows up the stuffed-shirt image that has plagued Wall Street for years. Videos feature money management and investment tips, live interviews, and a humorous take on contemporary news and entertainment. Free, ad-supported.

Sports fans will find a small but acceptable selection of programming thanks to ESPN. Watch for additions in the upcoming months...

Watch ESPN: Streams all of the ESPN products via simulcast, including ESPN, ESPN2, ESPN3, ESPNU, ESPNEWS, ESPN Deportes, Longhorn Network, ESPN Goal Line, and ESPN Buzzer Beater. Free add-on to your paid Watch ESPN subscription through your cable or satellite dish provider.

NBA Game Time: Includes live box scores, schedules and statistics for all NBA games, plus video highlights for each game. Free app, with a paid upgrade for the NBA League Pass so you can watch the games live.

Red Bull TV: Watch interviews, breaking news, and short and full-length movies on topics ranging from hockey to break dancing to motocross to extreme snowsports. Free, ad-supported.

And if you prefer your sports hands-on, instead of as a spectator...

Daily Burn: This well known smartphone workout app now has a workout video channel for Fire TV. Free for the first 30 days, then $10 monthly subscription.

MUSIC AND MUSIC VIDEOS

Music video fans will find the following offerings...

Qello Concerts: HD video footage of the world's greatest concerts, old and new, with every genre represented from rock to hip-hop to classical. Free basic subscription with paid VIP upgrade.

Vevo: The Internet's premiere music video site, with videos from two of three major record labels – a great alternative to MTV. Free, ad-supported.

Fire TV also supports Internet radio stations...

Pandora: The first open source Internet radio project with channels in every musical genre. The free version is ad-supported, with an ad-free paid upgrade.

iHeart Radio: A streaming compilation of all 800 Clear Channel radio stations in the US that you can use to create custom music stations of your own. Free, with live streaming stations supported by commercials. Custom music stations are currently commercial free.

TuneIn: Over 100,000 stations for live listening, plus 2 million on-demand radio programs including podcasts, concerts and interviews. Free, ad-supported.

GAMES

Amazon's promo page says there are 100 games available for the Fire TV, but we're already seeing more than that, and with an in-house game development team, they're in a good position to add at least one zero to that number within the upcoming year. (We cover the best of the Fire TV games in **Chapter 7**).

MEDIA ORGANIZERS AND STORAGE

Plex: This app stores all of your digital content in one place on its enormous cloud-based servers so you can access it from any device at any time. The Plex app for the Fire TV with basic features is currently on sale for 99 cents in the Amazon app store (normally it's $4.99). Buy the premium Plex Pass subscription to get the expanded features. (We cover Plex in depth in **Chapter 4**).

Frequency: This ad-supported app scours the Internet for videos and turns them into channels that you can watch on your Fire TV without queuing up each video separately. It automatically sorts through popular sites like Facebook, Twitter, CNN, the New York Times, National Geographic, Forbes, and more, plus you can add videos from your favorite websites and blogs. Frequency is especially handy for queuing up a batch of YouTube videos.

HEAD IN THE CLOUD...

...the Amazon Cloud, that is. Just what is Amazon Cloud? This file backup service lets you securely copy any file you own to your own little corner of Amazon's huge storage drives and download it back to your device at any time.

Your Fire TV can access your Amazon Cloud account to retrieve the movies, apps, games, photos, and personal videos you've stored there.

Simply scroll down the Main Menu and choose the media type you want to retrieve. The Fire TV will pull it down out of the Cloud.

When you open an account with Amazon, you automatically get 5 GB of free Cloud Drive storage for any type of media you upload to it. If you have a huge number of files that you want to back up, you can buy more storage from Amazon for a reasonable annual fee.

Better yet, any media you purchase from Amazon is automatically stored for free in your Amazon Cloud account, and it doesn't count against your 5 GB quota. The files you've stored in the Cloud are available at any time, on any Internet-connected device you own.

We explain how to retrieve them in the upcoming chapters on specific types of digital media, with a detailed explanation of how to upload your own files to your Amazon Cloud account in **Chapter 6**.

DELETING UNWANTED FILES FROM YOUR FIRE TV

Although you'll be streaming most of the movies and TV shows you watch on your Fire TV, games and apps are another story.

The Fire TV box needs to download a local copy of these files to its internal storage drive, and even though that drive is a generous 8 GB, it does fill up.

To uninstall a game or app, scroll down and select Settings on the Home screen's Main Menu and select the Applications sub-menu. Scroll down or up and select the app or game you want to delete. Select *Uninstall* and follow the prompts.

All of your Amazon purchased media is always available to download again from your Amazon Cloud account unless you deliberately delete it through your Amazon Cloud app (see **Chapter 6**) – which we recommend you don't do!

COMING SOON — AMAZON FREE TIME

Amazon's Free Time app for the Kindle Fire has been extremely popular, and a Fire TV version is being promised for the near future. Here's a summary of what's in store.

The basic Free Time app lets the user set up a custom library of Amazon content for up to six kids. With the paid upgrade to a monthly Free Time Unlimited subscription, Amazon will choose and deliver a custom-selected grab bag of children's videos, books, educational apps, movies, and television shows to your device.

Free Time is aimed at children ages 3 through 8 and is furnished by the major producers of kids' content, including Sesame Street, Disney, and Nickelodeon. You can even get content from PBS so your kids have a learning experience along with their entertainment.

We're watching for when this app becomes available for the Fire TV and will update this section accordingly when it does.

3. SETUP AND BASIC NAVIGATION

The word "easy" keeps popping up in Amazon's promotional copy for the Fire TV, and they're true to their promises – particularly when it comes to setting up the device. In fact, it's so easy that you can just follow the on-screen prompts and be looking at the Fire TV Home screen on your HDTV within minutes.

The quick start guide that comes in the box tells you everything you need to know and is available on Amazon's website if you ever lose it; just Google – **Amazon Fire TV User Guide – Amazon S3**.

The Amazon's Fire TV help videos are short, simple, and very well done. You can find them by googling *Amazon Fire TV Help Videos*

You can access on-screen help from the Fire TV Home screen by scrolling down the left sidebar and selecting *Settings*.

There are just a few things to keep in mind before you begin. First, you'll need a standard HDMI cable (male connector on both ends) to connect the Fire TV box to the HDMI port on your television and this cable is not included with the Fire TV package. You'll also need to use your television remote (not the Fire TV remote) to select HDMI as the input device for your HDTV.

Second, you have the choice of setting up your Fire TV to connect to the Internet with either an Ethernet cable (similar to a telephone jack cable, only bigger), or through your home wireless network if you have one.

Your Fire TV will automatically detect an Ethernet connection as soon as you plug in the cable, but if you go with wireless, then you'll need to enter your network password when the on-screen prompt comes up during the setup process.

Thanks to the voice search function on your Fire TV remote you won't need to 'type' in anything very often, but there are some instances where you will and entering the password for your wifi network when you first setup is one of them. When the the password prompt box appears just use the navigation wheel to move around the letters and numbers and the select button to enter them. Upper case letters can be found by selecting *ABC* and symbols by selecting *#$%*, and adding spaces or deleting a letter can be done more quickly using either the fast forward or rewind buttons on your remote if you prefer.

Amazon recommends that you place the Fire TV box out in the open if you're using a wireless connection – an enclosed cabinet will weaken its signal strength. We got a chuckle out of this – these devices are called "set-top boxes," but with an HDTV and wireless signal, there's no place to set them!

We also found out that if you want to switch over from an Ethernet connection to a wireless one, you'll have to disconnect the Ethernet cable from the Fire TV first to make the prompt come up to connect wirelessly.

If all goes well with the setup, you end up looking at the Fire TV Home screen with a colorful carousel of movie titles enticing you to start watching.

A ONE OF A KIND REMOTE

Amazon surprised everyone when it released the Fire TV with a voice activated remote. We love the voice activation; however, the most important button on the remote is the Select button, the unmarked center button inside the 5-way directional trackpad at the top of the remote.

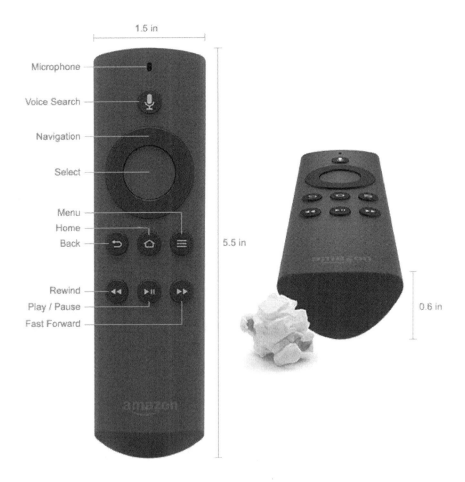

You'll use Select to choose options from the Home screen, while the raised ring around it lets you navigate up, down, left, and right, just like any other remote.

Below the trackpad you'll see the Back, Home, and Menu buttons, and below that are the Rewind, Play/Pause, and Forward buttons for controlling the video player.

The voice activation is only used for searching the Amazon media store for media titles. Simply press and hold the microphone button while you hold the remote 1 to 8 inches from your face, speak into it, and release the button when you're finished speaking to start the search.

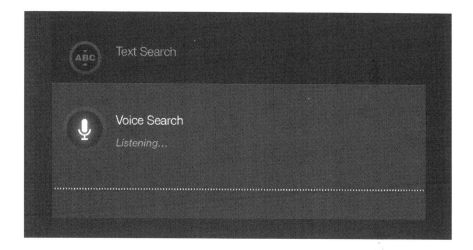

Keep background noise to a minimum for best results, and use short, descriptive keywords, because the voice recognition doesn't support natural language. Simply say a movie title, or an actor, character, or director's name, such as "The Graduate," or "Dustin Hoffman."

Don't ask questions like, "Where can I find movies from 1967?" Fire TV will display text of your search request on your TV screen and ask you to verify that the words are correct by pressing the Select button on the remote. When you get the results, use the remote's trackpad to scroll through them, and use the Select button to choose one.

If you can't get the results you want with voice search, simply press Up on the trackpad to open the text search menu and use the trackpad to key in your search term.

ANATOMY OF THE AMAZON FIRE TV BOX

There are five ports on the back of your Fire TV box.

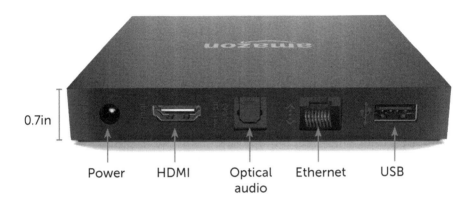

From left to right, they are...

Power: Connect to a wall outlet with the included power cord.

HDMI: Connect to the HDMI port on your HDTV (HDMI cable not included).

Optical audio: Optional connection to a stereo music system or home theater (audio cable not included).

Ethernet: If using a wired Internet connection, connect to your cable or DSL modem (Ethernet cable not included).

USB: Currently this port is unsupported – look for firmware upgrades in the near future.

There's no need to turn off or unplug your Fire TV – it automatically enters the sleep or screen saver mode if you stop using it for more than 30 minutes. Press any button on the remote to wake it up.

REGISTERING YOUR FIRE TV

When you purchase your Fire TV online from Amazon, it ships pre-registered to your Amazon.com buyer account, so there's no need to register the device at set-up.

The set-up process becomes just a bit more complicated if you're buying or selling one used, if you buy one from another retailer, or if someone purchased one on Amazon as a gift to you and forget to check off the box saying it's a gift before clicking the Buy button.

In these cases, you'll possibly need to deregister the device, and you'll definitely need to register it under your own account. To check the registration, use the remote to go to the Home screen. Use the down command on the remote to scroll to the bottom of the left sidebar menu. Select *Settings*; then select *My Account*.

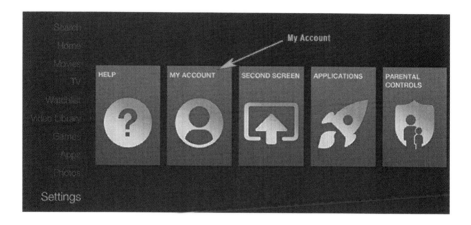

If the account listed doesn't match your own, select that account and select *Deregister*. You can then select *Register* to set up your Fire TV on your own Amazon account.

You also need to set up 1-Click Payment in your Amazon account from your computer, tablet, or smartphone Internet browser so you can make media purchases from the Amazon store.

You will need a credit card on file with Amazon to complete this task. Step away from the Fire TV and go to whatever device you use to browse the Internet.

Open a browser window and go to the Amazon.com website. Log in to your Amazon account and click the small black triangle next to *Your Account* under your name at the top right of the screen. Choose *Account Settings* from the Your Account page, scroll down, and click *1-Click Settings*. Go through the additional login and password screen and use the Edit button to enable 1-Click Payment.

GETTING TO KNOW THE HOME SCREEN

The Fire TV Home screen is the central headquarters for finding and playing all the media you've been waiting to watch. To get there at any time, simply press the *Home* button on the remote.

On the left side of the Home screen you'll see the Main Menu, which contains your content libraries and lets you control the settings for the Fire TV. Kindle Fire users will be pleased to see that the Main Menu is very similar to the Navigation Bar on the Kindle.

To scroll down the Main Menu, press *Down* on the remote. Press Up to scroll up, and press the Select button in the center of the navigation ring to select a highlighted menu item.

From top to bottom the menu items are...

Search: Opens the text search menu and keyboard for entering search terms with the remote, and provides a text display of what the Fire TV is hearing when you use voice commands to search.

Home: Returns you to the Home screen.

Movies: Browses the movie selections in the Amazon Instant Video store.

TV: Browses the TV episodes in Amazon Instant Video.

Watchlist: Displays media in the Amazon store and your Video Library (see below) that you've bookmarked to watch later.

Video Library: Displays movies and TV shows that you've already purchased from Amazon, which are automatically stored on your Amazon Cloud account for free (we explain Amazon Cloud in **Chapter 2**).

Games: Browses games available for streaming to the Fire TV.

Apps: Browses apps available for the Fire TV.

Photos: Browses your Amazon Cloud storage account for your personal photos and videos.

Settings: Sets custom functions on your Fire TV device.

We'll cover each category of Fire TV media on the Main Menu in depth separately in the upcoming chapters.

To the right of the Main Menu you'll find several rows of carousel items. These will change based on the type of media selected from the sidebar as well as your usage patterns, but we'll do a quick walk-through based on what you're most likely to see on your Home screen.

To enter the carousel area, press *Right* on the remote. To go back to the Main Menu, either press Left, or press the Back button.

The first carousel contains Recently Viewed items which you can select to watch again. As you scroll down the carousel rows, you will see Recommended Items based on your previous search history, New and Featured items that Amazon wants to promote, Bestsellers, and finally some selected categories based on Amazon's record of your interests.

To delete a title from the Recently Viewed carousel, use the remote's trackpad to navigate to that item and select it. Navigate to the Remove from Recent button below the item and press Select. You can also remove items from your Recommended Items list or Watchlist using similar commands. The rest of the carousel items can't be changed.

THE SETTINGS MENU

In addition to registering your device, there are a couple more items on the Settings submenu at the bottom of the Main Menu that you might need to visit at some point.

Help: A handy way to look up a process if you don't feel like getting up out of your chair and finding it on a computer.

My Account: In addition to registering and deregistering your device, this function syncs your Fire TV with your Amazon Cloud account so that all of your Amazon purchases are available for streaming.

Second Screen: Enables the Fire TV to connect with a compatible tablet like the Kindle Fire HDX tablet and mirror its screen on your HDTV. Second Screen also lets you use your tablet to explore information about a movie or TV show on the Internet Movie Database (IMDb) through Amazon's X-ray while you watch that show on your Fire TV.

Applications: Controls several functions in your apps and games. If you have trouble stopping an app that runs in the background after you close the app, which is common with radio channels, use the *Force Stop* command in this submenu to quit the app.

You can also delete downloaded applications here – rest assured that they are always available to download again from your Amazon Cloud account where all of your purchased media is stored. However, some saved data like game scores, may be permanently deleted.

Parental Controls: Uses password protection to restrict access to certain content on your Fire TV. You can also block media purchases and in-app upgrades so an unauthorized user or exuberant teenager won't max out your credit card shopping in the Amazon store.

Note that Parental Controls will only restrict access to media titles in Amazon's store. Restriction of media in apps like Netflix must be done from within the app itself.

Navigate to the **Settings** menu and scroll across to **Parental Controls** and select it. By default Parental Controls will be 'OFF' and you should tap the OFF button to activate the feature. You will immediately be prompted to enter and then reconfirm a 5 digit PIN. Once done you will now see further options.

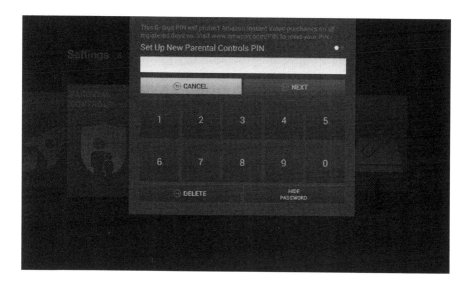

You can, of course, turn off Parental Controls again, which will require you to enter your PIN first. You can also set either **PIN Protect Purchases** or **PIN Protect Amazon Video**, the first option will require you to enter your PIN for *any* Amazon purchases and the second option will require you to enter your PIN just for Amazon Instant Video purchases.

Block Content Types allows you to block hand pick content from being viewed without first entering your PIN and **Change PIN** is for changing your PIN number, but will require you to enter your old PIN first.

Should you forget your Amazon Instant Video PIN number then you can reset it from your Amazon user account screen in your web browser at **http://amazon.com/PIN**.

Controllers: Pairs Bluetooth compatible game controllers with the Fire TV.

System: sets up a screen saver and connects the Fire TV with your home wireless network.

A WORD ABOUT AUDIO SETTINGS

You will also find within the **System** section of your settings menu an **Audio** setup section. By default your Fire TV will be set to output audio through both your HDMI and optical audio outputs in stereo sound quality. If you have the right TV or audio equipment you have a further option to enable Dolby Digital Plus sound. Just navigate to the Audio section within System settings then scroll to **Dolby Digital Output** and select it, you will then have the option to turn on Dolby Digital Plus for either your TV or audio device (HDMI or optical audio depending on how you are connected).

However a word of warning, Dolby Digital Plus is a very specific type of Dolby sound quality and if your TV or audio equipment is not comaptible with Dolby Digital Plus you won't hear anything at all! Furthermore if, for example, you are watching a movie from Amazon Instant Video then it too needs to have a Dolby Digital soundtrack. If you change your Audio settings and lose sound then please return to the section and reset it to the default "off" position.

MIRRORING YOUR KINDLE FIRE HDX SCREEN

Amazon developed the Kindle Fire HDX with the capability to "fling" its screen image to mirror on smart TV devices, and it expanded that capability to the Fire TV when the device was released. Note that earlier Kindle Fire models and the smaller 7" Fire HD don't support screen mirroring on the Fire TV.

To mirror your Kindle Fire HDX screen to your HDTV, start by activating the Fire TV's Second Screen setting from the Settings menu as described in the previous section. Note that both the Kindle and the Fire TV must be turned on and connected to the Internet, preferably on the same wireless network, and registered to the same Amazon user account.

You should also enable location-based services from the Settings menu on your Kindle so the familiar pop-up window doesn't stop your video cold while trying to find your location. We have tried and failed to disable that annoying pop-up, but nobody seems to know how to do it.

Next, on your Kindle, swipe down, tap *Settings*, and tap the *Display Settings* submenu. Look for *Display Mirroring*, tap it, and wait for the Kindle to detect your Fire TV.

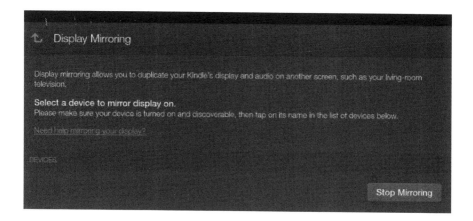

When the Fire TV device name appears, tap it. After about 30 seconds you should see an exact mirror on your HDTV of whatever appears on your Kindle screen. Now just find something you want to watch on your Kindle and play it.

If you can't get a good mirror, try starting your video before activate the mirroring from the Settings menu, instead of after. Mirroring is ideal if you want to watch channels like HBO Go, which the Fire TV doesn't support, but the Kindle does.

You can also mirror your Silk Browser window, presentations from apps like Office Suite Professional, and numerous games that are available for the Kindle but not for the Fire TV. To stop mirroring, swipe down from the top and use the Settings menu to end the process.

If you don't own a Kindle Fire HDX, screen mirroring support for Android devices is available by downloading the AllCast app to your smartphone or tablet from the **Google Play app store**.

4. WATCHING MOVIES AND TV SHOWS

There are two ways to watch movies and TV episodes on the Fire TV: you can stream or download them directly from Amazon's video store, or you can subscribe to a channel, download its app, and get access to that channel's content library. In this chapter we explain how to do both.

BUY OR RENT SHOWS FROM AMAZON

The Amazon Instant Video store is the source of all the splashy content you see on your Fire TV's Home screen. Here you can buy or rent movies and TV videos à la carte, one title at a time, and pay for them with 1-click ordering in your Amazon account.

Buying à la carte assures you of getting the titles you want, when you want them. The movies and TV episodes you buy are yours to watch on any device you own, including a laptop, smartphone, tablet, and of course your Fire TV.

Pricing in Amazon's movie and TV store ranges from $12.99 to buy new movie and TV releases to $4.99 for older titles. HD versions of some movies are available for a $5.00 upcharge.

You can stream your purchased titles directly from their permanent storage spot in Amazon's Cloud server, or download them your Fire TV or other device.

Rentals are either $3.99 or $2.99 depending on the age of the show, with some HD titles available for a $1.00 upcharge. The rental period for video content is only 48 hours, but it doesn't begin until you actually start to watch the video and you typically have up to 30 days to start watching.

You don't need to return a rental video – it simply becomes unavailable when the rental period expires. Another handy thing about Amazon!

To start browsing in the Amazon Instant Video store, use the remote to scroll down to either Movies or TV on the Main Menu in the Home screen and select one of them. The carousels to the right will display several subcategories for you to scroll through and choose from, using the trackpad's right and left buttons.

You can also search for particular titles, actors, directors, and types of videos using the voice command on the remote, or with a text search (**see Chapter 3**). Press *Select* to pick a video out of the line-up.

If you have the $99 annual Amazon Prime membership, then you can stream your pick of 40,000 Prime Instant Video titles to your Fire TV – for free! Some Prime Instant titles are even available to download for offline viewing.

Prime members will see the blue and yellow Prime badge in the upper left corner of any carousel items that are available for free. There's also a carousel row for Top Prime Movies and TV that you can use to search for those coveted freebies.

To buy or rent any movie or TV show, select the title to display its product page. You'll see a brief summary of the show and a row of

buttons underneath. These buttons enable you to buy the show, to rent it if it's available for rental, to add it to your Watchlist, or to watch its trailer.

Selecting the *More Ways to Watch* button displays pricing for HD versions if they are available, and sometimes the option to watch the video through a channel subscription.

To buy or rent a title, select the buy or rent option you prefer and then select the *Buy Now* button to give Amazon permission to charge your credit card with 1-Click Payment (**see Chapter 3**).

When your purchase is complete, you'll be given the option to select *Watch Now*. If you want to watch your purchase later, simply navigate to another menu item while Amazon immediately stores your video permanently in your Cloud account for access at any time.

To play a video from your Cloud account, you can select it from the Fire TV carousel if you've recently watched or purchased it, or you can find it by scrolling down the Main Menu on the Home screen and selecting *Video Library* to display all of your stored Amazon videos. Select the artwork for the one you want and it will start to play immediately.

Note that rentals and free Prime Instant Videos are not stored in your Cloud account, since you don't own them. However, you will see carousel rows on your Fire TV's Home screen for Recently Viewed and Recently Added to Prime, which will save you from having to hunt for them if you want to watch them again.

Also remember that you can always add any video to your Watchlist by selecting that button on its product page. To access your Watchlist, use the trackpad to scroll down the *Main Menu* and select it.

The *Play/Pause, Forward,* and *Rewind* buttons toward the bottom of the remote give you some great options for controlling your movie and TV show playback. Play/Pause is a "toggle" button – press it once to pause the video; press it again to release the pause.

Pressing the *Rewind* or *Forward* button once allows you to skip 10 seconds backward or forward. You can also press and hold the *Rewind* or *Forward* button to keep going backward or forward in the video, while additional presses allow you to cycle through the available speed options.

USING SECOND SCREEN FUNCTIONALITY

If you have a Kindle Fire HDX, you can use the Second Screen feature to "fling" your Kindle's screen image to the Fire TV and leaving you free to do other things on your HDX.

One of the other things you can do is learn more about the movie or TV show you're watching by exploring it on your Kindle with X-Ray, powered by IMDb. You'll get an uncluttered display of the show on your HDTV, while your Kindle lets you dive deep in-scene to explore characters, trivia, music, and more.

To activate Second Screen don't forget to turn this feature on in your Fire TV settings as previously discussed. Then go to the Video store on your Kindle HDX and select the movie or TV show you want to watch. Look for the *Send To* icon embedded in the Watch button on the product page and select it.

Your show will start to play on your Kindle, mirrored on your HDTV while you use your Kindle to explore its X-ray data and control play/pause, volume, and fast forward.

You can also use your Kindle to check your email, look at your personal photos, read a book, or surf the Internet while using it as a movie player for your Fire TV. Multitasking at its best!

SUBSCRIBE TO A CHANNEL AND GET UNLIMITED VIEWING

With the channel subscriptions like Netflix, you download an app to your Fire TV and use it to find and watch unlimited content in that channel's library. In some cases you'll need to pay for a subscription to a particular channel, while other channels are completely free. There are others that are free but allow you to pay to eliminate advertising.

Channel subscriptions begin with selecting the *App* option from the Main Menu on the Fire TV home screen. This will change the carousel to display new and popular app selections, as well as any apps you've recently used.

Finding the app you want is almost exactly like shopping in the Amazon Instant Video Store. For example, if you want to download and install the Netflix app on your Fire TV, you can use either the voice command on the remote, or a text search.

Select the Netflix app artwork to bring up its product screen, and click the *Buy* button to begin downloading. Most channel apps are free to download, and you can pay for the few paid apps you'll need for your Fire TV with your Amazon Coins as well as your 1-Click Payment method. (**See below** to learn about Amazon Coins.)

You'll see an Open button to start using the app right away, or if you don't, the app will be safely stored in your Amazon Cloud account. To uninstall an app, scroll down and select Settings on the Home screen's Main Menu and select the Applications submenu. Scroll down or up and select the app you want to delete. Select *Uninstall* and follow the prompts.

For channels that charge a subscription fee, you will need to enable an in-app purchase and pay for it with a credit card. An in-app purchase is an upgrade that unlocks that channel's content library for unlimited viewing through the app.

Although Amazon says you can pay for these with 1-click payment or Amazon Coins (**see below**), in practice we've found this is rarely possible since the channel providers are outside of Amazon's content ecosystem.

The first step for an in-app purchase is usually registering an account with your email address and password, followed by keying in your name, address, and credit card number. While these purchases are generally secure, entering the data with the Fire TV remote can be pretty tedious.

We prefer to register and subscribe from our laptop's web browser so we can do it with a real keyboard. Simply type the channel's name (e.g., Netflix) into a search engine like Google or Bing.

Go to its home page and look for a link that says "Register," or in the case of Netflix, "Not a member? Click here."

Be sure to record your user name and password somewhere so you don't lose them. Once you've registered and paid up, you can go back to your Fire TV, log in once with your user name and password, and you shouldn't have to do it again.

If anything, playing movies and TV shows on a Fire TV channel is even easier than making an à la carte purchase from Amazon Instant Video.

If you've used the channel's app recently, it will show up in the *Recently Viewed* carousel on your Fire TV Home screen. If you haven't used it lately, you can find it in your Amazon Cloud account by scrolling down the Main Menu and selecting *Apps*. Select the *Your Apps Library* submenu, and look for the app you want amongst all of your apps purchased on Amazon.

Select the app's artwork to open it and look for movies or TV episodes to watch. Most channels, including Netflix, use a carousel-style menu similar to the one on your Fire TV home screen. Use the trackpad to scroll left or right and to move up and down from row to row. Select the artwork for any title to immediately start playing it.

There are some things that channel subscriptions can't do on the Fire TV. Voice command searching doesn't work within channel apps since they don't use Amazon's search engine, so you'll have to resort to text searching if you're looking for a specific title.

Also keep in mind that channels are for streaming only, so you can't download any shows from them, and they don't store your show selections in your Amazon Cloud account.

AMAZON COINS — PLAY MONEY!

Coins? Has Amazon gotten so huge that they're printing their own money? Well, yes. Coins are Amazon's virtual money that you can buy with your real money and spend on apps, games, and some in-app upgrades. Amazon has a generous "exchange rate" – one Coin is worth one US penny, but the more coins you buy at once, the bigger your discount, anywhere from 4 to 10 percent.

You also earn extra coins as an incentive for buying certain apps and games, and when you activate your Fire TV, Amazon gives you a nice 1,000 Coin deposit to get you started.

When you use your Fire TV, Android device, or Kindle to shop for a game or app, the product page will display the Coin price as well as the regular price, any Coin bonuses for purchase, and how many coins you have left in your account.

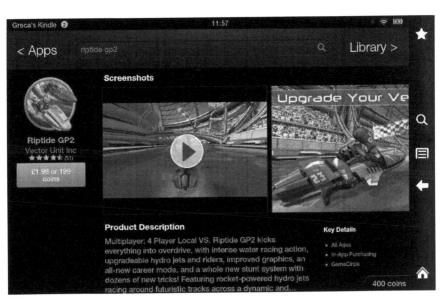

To buy more coins for your account, say "Amazon Coins" into the remote mic, or press Up and use the remote to type those words into the text search menu. You'll be able to buy as many coins as you need with your 1-click ordering account on Amazon.

MANAGING CLOSED CAPTIONS

It's easy to watch a video that offers closed captions. Movies and TV in the Amazon Instant Video Store are marked with a small "CC" icon on the product page if closed captioning is available.

Start by selecting the show you want to watch and playing it. Then press the *Menu* button on the remote. A menu will appear on your screen and you can simply select *Turn Captions On*. Then use the trackpad to choose text size and color for the caption text.

Press *Menu* again to resume playback with captions enabled. You can turn captions off by pressing the *Menu* button on the remote and selecting *Turn Captions Off*.

Netflix lets you change your caption settings from your computer, tablet, or smartphone web browser by going to Subtitle Appearance at **www.netflix.com/youraccount**. Other Fire TV channels also may allow you to set up captioning if you do a bit of browsing around on their websites.

USING PLEX TO PUT YOUR LOCAL CONTENT ON YOUR FIRE TV

It's inevitable that sooner or later you'll want to play some locally stored non-Amazon content from another device on your Fire TV, and unfortunately, Amazon doesn't make it easy for you to do that.

We would really like to see a Main Menu option allowing us to access our entire Amazon Cloud storage account, where we've backed up our entire music and video library from our personal collection of CDs and our iTunes account for our Mac laptops.

Alas, at this time only our Amazon-purchased content plus personal photos and home video are available from Amazon Cloud on our Fire TV.

Enter Plex, a super-smart media storage app that backs up any content from any device you own on its enormous hard drives and stores it securely for you to access with the Plex app.

There's a version of this app for just about every device on the market, including the Fire TV. This means you can upload your entire media collection from your computer's hard drive to Plex, and then stream it on your Fire TV through the Plex app.

Like that really smart kid you remember from school, Plex can be a bit intimidating, but don't be put off. You're not going to lose any data if you use it, so why not give it a whirl? We did, and we're hooked.

It's best to start with one simple uploading task, which for us was getting our iTunes library uploaded from our Mac laptop so we could play our songs on our Fire TV. Windows users will find the process is almost identical, and we've noted below where it's different.

Your first step is to scroll down the Fire TV's Main Menu and open the Amazon app store. Search for the Plex app using voice command or text search, buy it, and install it. You don't need to open it just yet.

Next, go to the device where the local content you want to upload to Plex is stored. For us, that was our MacBook Pro. Use your web browser to navigate to the **Plex.tv** home page.

Click the *Sign Up* button at the top right and register your information. You'll get an email asking you to click a link to confirm your registration. Be sure to record your user name and password for future reference.

Click the *Launch* button in the top right corner to go to the download page and install the Plex app for your computer.

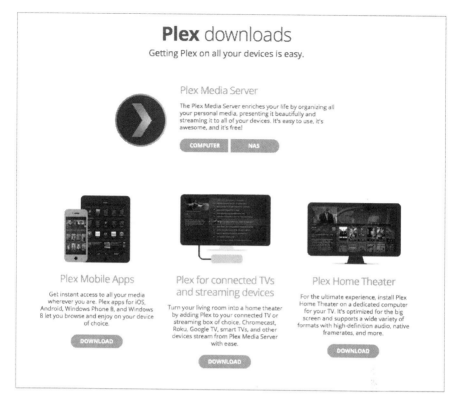

Note that you can also download an app for your tablet or smartphone from this page if that's where your local media is stored, but we downloaded the app for Mac OS. It's a big .zip file that goes to your Downloads folder.

When downloading is complete, click it open and drag the app to your Applications folder. (Windows users will put it in Programs.)

The next part is not exactly intuitive, but we just kept following the prompts and it turned out great. You need to add at least one library to your Plex account so there's a place on their storage drives to hold your media files.

Click the *Add Library* button. The app will ask you to choose a type of media from a set of graphic icons.

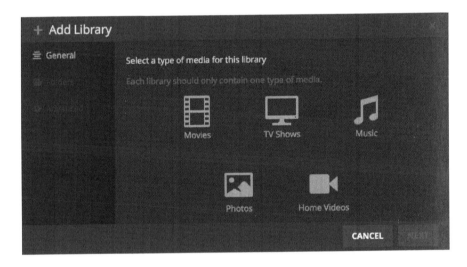

We chose Music for our iTunes library.

Now Plex will want to you to show it the folder where you keep the media you want to upload. This is fairly easy on both a Mac and Windows computer since both operating systems have clearly labeled folders for music, videos, and photos.

We selected the Music folder on our Mac and then chose the iTunes library. Whoosh, suddenly our entire music collection was uploading to Plex. Success!

Back on your Fire TV, you'll need to find and open the Plex app from *Your Apps Library* under *Apps* on the Main Menu.

Log in with your Plex user name and password – the only time you will need to do this. Select *My Library* from the menu bar at the top, and with any luck you will see a little gold Plex icon with a label for the library you just uploaded from your computer.

Select this icon and scroll through the album artwork from your iTunes account to find your music and play it on your Fire TV.

Plex will also upload and play videos and photos on your Fire TV, plus it's a great place to store any content you value and don't want to lose. It's a fantastic app with far more capabilities than we've described here, but those are beyond the scope of the Fire TV.

However, we encourage you to explore it further, and so does Plex – they're offering a $4.00 discount on their app for the Fire TV to celebrate Amazon's release of the product.

5. MUSIC VIDEO AND RADIO

Music lovers won't go hungry for long with the Fire TV. Already Amazon has negotiated channel agreements with two music video companies and three Internet radio providers, giving you thousands of concerts and millions of songs to choose from.

It's well worth owning the Fire TV simply to get your audio off the small speakers on your tablet or laptop and onto your HDTV where the sound quality is better.

You can even use your Fire TV as a radio playing in the background – it allows you to return to the Home screen at any time while it keeps playing your music selections, allowing you to browse the Amazon media stores, play games, and share photos. The powerful Fire TV box is robust enough to handle all of these tasks at once.

MUSIC VIDEO CHANNELS

Music video streaming is a natural for the Fire TV. There's nothing quite as dynamic as a good live concert viewed in HD, especially if your HDTV has a good sound system. Here's a look at the Fire TV's two music video channels.

Qello Concerts: This premium music video channel offers something to please just about everyone.

Just browsing around in their categories, we found concert footage of the early Beatles, jazz genius Miles Davis, the Sleeping Beauty opera by the Royal Ballet, and Pink Floyd live at Knebworth.

Qello's emphasis is on contemporary music, but if you have a wide range of tastes, as we do, then their library will keep you busy for a good long time. Registration is required even for their free account, but it's easy enough to do from directly from your Fire TV screen using the remote to key in your email and password.

The really good stuff is only accessible for their $4.99 a month upgrade, but if you click away from the purchase screen, they'll offer you 25 percent off your subscription – not a bad deal at all.

Vevo: This music video site will remind you of MTV, and in fact it's their biggest competitor. Choose from Vevo's 24/7 streaming music video channel, or browse through their library of over 75,000 music videos.

This library doesn't have a very robust search function – it doesn't let you search by category – and the home screen display is definitely aimed at the youth market.

However, we found plenty of great stuff for more "mature" audiences through searching by artist and keyword; it just took a bit of patience to type in all those keystrokes with the remote. Vevo is free, supported by 30 second ad spots before the video starts. Registration is simple enough to key in with the Fire TV remote.

RADIO STATION CHANNELS

Amazon has partnered with three big players from the world of Internet radio with dedicated apps for the Fire TV. Their interfaces are fairly similar, so we'll give you some general pointers for turning your Fire TV into a radio.

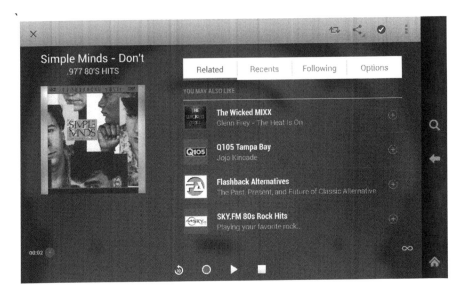

The Fire TV's three music-only channels use a layout similar to your Fire TV, with categories to the left and suggestions to the right. In the left sidebar, you can choose a musical genre, which will change the suggestions displayed in the right column.

Pandora and iHeart Radio also give you the option of building one or more custom song lists from their available music libraries, which they call custom stations. This process is less frustrating if you do it from a device with at least an on-screen keyboard, so we recommend downloading the app to your smartphone, tablet, or Kindle Fire before you play around with building your own stations.

Pandora: This Internet radio project was doing social media before it was cool. Begin by registering a free account, which is easy enough to do from your Fire TV. You'll be presented with the option of making your song list public, which allows you to actually create your own radio station, but you can remain private if you like.

If you don't feel up to the task of building your own station, you can browse through a huge selection of genres containing radio stations created by other Pandora users. One of the things we really like about this app is its sleep timer and alarm clock features. The paid upgrade to Pandora One is $3.99 monthly to get rid of the pop-up ads.

iHeart Radio: The media giant Clear Channel has compiled its 800 US radio stations into a single channel for the Fire TV. You can either listen live to one of more of these stations, or compile their content into your own custom music stations and share them with your friends.

iHeart doesn't require registration, and there's no paid upgrade. You'll see video ads on the live stations, but your custom music stations are currently commercial free while this new service gets off the ground. This Fire TV channel also has a sleep timer and alarm clock.

TuneIn: Enjoy live listening on over 100,000 Internet radio stations, including big names like CBS, ESPN, NPR, C-SPAN, and a nice selection of international stations. You'll also get access to 2 million archived podcasts, concerts and interviews.

Registration is required and is easy to do from the Fire TV. TuneIn has an easy to use interface that allows you to set favorites. It's free and ad-supported, but the scrolling banner ad bar at the bottom of the screen is completely tolerable. Not only that, but for a one-time $3.99 fee, you can record anything you hear on TuneIn – the only restriction is that you can't share the recording.

COMING SOON — AMAZON MP3 LIBRARY

Coming soon, you'll be able to stream your complete MP3 music library from Amazon Cloud storage, as long as you purchased those songs on Amazon. This will include CDs you bought, as well as the songs you downloaded.

This section of the book will be updated accordingly when the feature is released. In the meantime, take a look at the Plex app for the Fire TV (**see Chapter 4**) if you want to stream your music collection on your Fire TV.

6. PHOTOS AND PERSONAL VIDEOS

With the release of the Fire TV, Amazon was smart enough to recognize that other digital media players had weaknesses when it comes to playing local content.

By "local," we mean content that you've stored on one of your devices, such as the hard drive on your desktop or laptop computer, or in the limited Flash memory that comes installed on a tablet or smartphone.

Although the Fire TV doesn't play all types of local content, it does let you stream your photos and personal videos, as long as you've uploaded them to your Amazon Cloud account.

LIFE SIZE MEMORIES

The Fire TV is tailor made for a family photo or video viewing session on your HDTV, but first you'll have to install Amazon's Cloud Drive application on your computer.

Go to **http://www.amazon.com/gp/drive/app-download** and let the site automatically detect which version you need before it presents you with a download. You can also click *Your Cloud Drive* from the drop-down menu under Your Account on the Amazon home screen and install the application from there.

Open and install the downloaded file to your hard drive. This application will then let you connect to Cloud Drive with your computer so you can upload and download up to 2 GB of data with a simple drag-and-drop interface.

If you install it on your tablet or smartphone, it will automatically upload any photos and videos you shoot within seconds, so they'll be immediately available for streaming to your Fire TV. The Cloud Drive app also syncs your content across all of your devices, so you'll always be up to date.

To upload content from your computer to Amazon Cloud Drive, open the Cloud Drive app that you've just installed, you can find it by clicking *Start*, then *All Programs* on Windows or in the Applications folder on a Mac. Once you open the app you'll see a Cloud Drive folder with several subfolders for different types of media.

Simply drag and drop any media you want into one of the folders and it will automatically upload to your Amazon Cloud account. To download it back to your computer, open the Cloud Drive folder and drag the file out of its folder and onto your hard drive.

If you only have a small number of local files to store, and they're not too big, you can just upload your content straight into your Cloud Drive account via your browser.

Go to the main Amazon Cloud Drive page at **https://www.amazon. com/clouddrive**

Sign in, and instead of clicking on "Install Cloud Drive" click on *"Continue to your Cloud Drive"* located at the top right of the page.

Once there you will see your content subfolders, and by clicking *Upload*, you can browse your computer for the relevant content you wish to store.

Once you've uploaded your local content to your Amazon Cloud account, you can view it on your Fire TV by scrolling down the Fire TV Main Menu and selecting Photos to stream your personal photos and videos to your HDTV.

Your Cloud Drive account also contains a record of every digital file you've ever purchased from Amazon (including free apps and games). We strongly recommend that you **NEVER** delete these files, or you'll have to pay for them again if you need to download them to one of your devices.

VIEW SLIDESHOWS

The Fire TV has a built-in slideshow function inside the Photos submenu on the Main menu. Start by selecting Photos from the Home Screen. Amazon Cloud organizes your photos into albums, so all you have to do is select one of them from the Photos submenu and then select *Start Slideshow*.

The slideshow advances automatically through your album, but you can use the remote's trackpad to go forward or back at your own pace.

USING SECOND SCREEN TO MIRROR PHOTOS AND VIDEOS FROM YOUR KINDLE

If you have a Kindle Fire HDX, you can use the Second Screen feature to "fling" your personal photos and videos stored on your e-reader to your Fire TV. Tap *Photos* on the Navigation Bar to open your photo library.

Then swipe from left to right to select a category or album. Look for the *Send To* icon ⬆ indicating that Second Screen is available to use.

Tap it, and the photo album on your Kindle will display on your HDTV.

SET UP A SCREEN SAVER

Your Fire TV automatically goes into sleep mode after 30 minutes with no activity. If you want to customize its screen saver display, you can set up one of your photo albums in your Amazon Cloud account as your personal screen saver.

From the Home screen, select **Photos** from the Main Menu, and then select **Add Photos and Videos**. Choose the photo album you want to display, and then select **Set as Screen Saver**.

You can customize the style, speed, and start time for the slideshow from the Fire TV Settings menu on the Home screen. Select the **System** submenu, and then select **Screen Saver**. Within this section you can **Preview** your current screen saver, select **Album** to choose a different album of photos or the default Amazon Collection. Select **Shuffle** to show the photos in your album in a random order, select **Slide Style** to choose the way one photo transitions into another and select **Slide Speed** to set the speed with which photos change. Finally selecting **Start Time** allows you to determine how long your Fire TV is idle for before your screen saver starts.

7. GAMES IN THE WORKS

Everything about the Fire TV declares its edge over its competitors when it comes to games. Although the device can't beat the dedicated gaming devices like the PlayStation or Xbox for speed and variety, it's going to be a great, inexpensive option for families who want to play some simple games, particularly those with younger children.

A month after the release, the selection had already grown to 150 game titles, with more being added every day. Many of them originate with Amazon's in-house game development department, which is working to develop games specifically for the Fire TV.

To sweeten the deal and bring as many users on board as possible, virtually all games for the Fire TV are either free, or under $5.00.

To see the Fire TV games store, scroll down the Main Menu on the Home screen and select *Games* to browse by category or access the carousel displays. Click the artwork for the game you want to start playing it.

If your game requires a controller device and you don't have one connected, you'll see a warning on the purchase screen that you need it to play the game.

To uninstall a game, scroll down and select *Settings* on the Home screen's Main Menu and select the *Applications* submenu. Scroll down or up, and select the game you want to delete. Select *Uninstall* and follow the prompts.

If you want to block your household's resident gamer from buying paid upgrades to a particular game (or all of them) on your Fire TV, follow the instructions for setting up **Parental Controls in Chapter 3**.

GAME CONTROLLER PAIRING

Amazon has developed a nice, reasonably priced game controller device specifically for the Fire TV that you can order from its online store. The controller doesn't come bundled with the Fire TV and must be ordered separately, but Amazon gives you a nice $10 bonus for ordering in the form of a 1,000 deposit of Amazon Coins in your account. (**See Chapter 4** to learn about Amazon Coins.)

To pair your Amazon controller with your Fire TV, install the controller's batteries so it powers on and then hold down the Home button for 5 seconds. You will see the four status lights on the unit flashing back and forth two at a time, signaling that pairing is available.

Next, on your Fire TV, select *Settings* from the Main Menu and select the *Bluetooth Controllers* submenu. Select *Add New Controller* and choose *Amazon Fire game controller* from the list of available devices. Watch the four status lights carefully until all of them light up at once, showing that pairing succeeded. After 6 seconds they will go off completely.

You can also pair your controller with your Kindle Fire and take advantage of the larger game selection for the Kindle. If your Kindle is an HDX model, you can mirror the game to your Fire TV (**see Chapter 3**), greatly expanding its gaming capabilities.

Some Fire TV games will also work with other, non-Amazon controllers that run on Bluetooth, and some games can be played with the Fire TV remote alone. To see the capabilities of each game, select its artwork from the Games submenu on the Main Menu. On its product page, look in the Works With box to see what kind of options you have for controlling that game on your Fire TV.

GAMECIRCLE

The GameCircle function lets you share your Fire TV gaming milestones in a public profile, including your game scores, times, and major victories. You and all other members of your Circle can see each other's GameCircle profiles, adding a social dimension to Fire TV gaming.

You can use GameCircle to set up your profile, view other users' profiles, and send and receive invitations to join any GameCircle.

To share data through GameCircle, the game you're playing must be GameCircle enabled. Select a game from the Fire TV's Games submenu to open it, and then press either the *Home* button on your remote, or the *GameCircle* button on the Amazon game controller.

GameCircle Button

If you see a Welcome Back message, you'll know GameCircle is enabled for that game.

To hide your GameCircle profile, select *Settings* from the Main Menu, and select the *Applications* submenu. Select Amazon GameCircle, and set Share Your GameCircle Nickname to *Off*.

Your profile will be completely hidden, and you won't be able to participate in any circles until you reactivate it. However, your gaming data will remain stored in your account unless you delete your profile entirely.

AVAILABLE GAMES FOR THE FIRE TV

Although the selection isn't huge as of yet, there are some amazingly sophisticated games in the Fire TV line-up. Here are a few of the best-known highlights; you will download them dirrectly through your Amazon TV but we include the links to Amazon.com here should you wish to look them up on your computer or tablet.

Quell: This gorgeously designed puzzle game features 80 levels of play, 3D graphics, and a fascinating soundtrack by composer Steven Cravis. Don't be fooled by its New Age packaging – this game is extremely challenging and will give your gray matter a real workout.

Sonic the Hedgehog series: Lace up your running shoes and join the world's fastest animated hedgehog as he races through complex 3D environments and eludes his competitors and enemies while making new friends along the way.

Despicable Me: Team up with the Minions, the animated townsfolk of Gru, who carry out challenging missions in 3D animation to commit despicable acts. Be sure to check out the Fluffy Unicorn!

Walking Dead: Based on the award-winning comic book series, this game throws life and death decisions at you as you watch Lee, a hardened ex-con, protect a young girl in a world full of zombies that have come back to life.

Ashphalt 8: A thrilling 3D animated auto racing game for those who can't get enough horsepower in real life. Fantastic special effects, along with barrel rolls, jumps, and speed, speed, and more speed.

Minecraft-Pocket Edition: Build brave new worlds with this simulation game with two modes for two extremes: survival, starting with nothing; and creative, starting with everything. This sophisticated game series is a bit pricier than the others at $6.99.

Riptide GP2: Ride a rocket powered water jet machine around a watery obstacle course at high speeds and show off your outlandish stunt mastery. GameCircle enabled so you can share and compete with your friends.

Monsters University: It's back to school time at Disney / Pixar studio's dear old MU. Get acquainted with Mike, Sulley, and Squishy, and chase Archie the Scare Pig around as he squeals and tries to get away.

8. TROUBLESHOOTING

Trouble with the Fire TV is fairly rare. Most of the issues seem to occur with third-party devices and apps from outside of the Amazon system. Here we've tried to focus on problems you're mostly likely to experience and offer some easy fixes.

BASIC TROUBLESHOOTING

For the catch-all category of errors such as frozen screens, apps that hang, or media that won't play, try the first step of simply resetting the Fire TV box. Disconnect the power cord, wait at least three seconds, and plug it back in.

If a particular app for the Fire TV is giving you problems, try changing its settings. Select *Settings* from the Main Menu, select *Applications*, and select the troublesome app. There are several actions you can take from here, from clearing its data, to force stopping it, to uninstalling it entirely and then reinstalling it.

One of these fixes usually works; however, any saved information may be lost, including your winning game scores.

If you can't connect to the Amazon store to browse or buy content, make sure you have an active Internet connection for your Fire TV. From the Main Menu, select *Settings*, select the *System* submenu, and select *Wi-Fi* to make sure your connection is working.

Problems with purchasing or accessing content can be solved by enabling or re-enabling your 1-Click Payment settings (**see Chapter 3**). You should also make sure your Fire TV box is registered to the right Amazon account.

From the Main Menu, select *Settings* and then select *My Account*. If you don't see your account, you'll need to deregister and reregister your Fire TV (**see Chapter 3**).

PROBLEMS CONNECTING TO WI-FI

Wireless Internet signals can be troublesome from time to time. If the Settings menu on your Fire TV shows you have no wireless connection, first make sure your Fire TV box is out in the open where the signal won't be blocked.

Disconnect and reconnect the power cord to reset the device before you continue. Also, sometimes your wireless router or modem will spontaneously disconnect.

Try restarting them both at once by unplugging them to trigger a reset. If your other wireless devices are connecting, though, then the router or modem isn't the problem.

Make sure you have entered the right password for your wireless network. This password isn't the same as your Amazon account password. If you're not sure, go to Wi-Fi in the Settings menu and re-enter it.

Finally, you can try connecting your Fire TV to the Internet with an Ethernet cable. If it suddenly connects, then you know the problem is with your wireless network, not the Fire TV or your Internet connection.

After this test, go back to the Settings menu to reactivate your Fire TV's wireless connection – but be sure to unplug the Ethernet cable first.

Your Fire TV has pretty conventional requirements for a wireless connection, but if you're not technically inclined, you might not know the specs for your wireless router.

Look on the case on the underside of your router and get name and model number; then look it up on the Internet. The Fire TV requires the following router specs:

- Open, WEP, WPA/WPA2 PSK, or WPA/WPA2 EAP encrypted network.
- B, G, and N routers on 2.4Ghz or A and N routers on 5Ghz.

If your router doesn't match these specs (probably because it's too old), then you'll have to buy and install a new one.

IF YOU CAN'T PAIR YOUR REMOTE OR GAME CONTROLLER

The Fire TV remote's pairing with the box is automatic as soon as you install the batteries. The Amazon game controller has to be paired manually, but it's a simple matter of pressing and holding the controller's Home button for 5 seconds (**see Chapter 7**).

If the box is unresponsive to the remote or controller, press and hold the Home button for 5 seconds and try again within 5 minutes, before the Fire TV goes into sleep mode.

Make sure the remote or controller batteries are fresh, and that you're within 30 feet of the Fire TV unit. Also make sure the Fire TV box is out in the open so the signal isn't blocked.

9. THE FIRE TV NEXT TIME

The development process for the Fire TV was conducted with such stealth that some tasks remained unfinished on its April 2, 2014, launch date.

It's only logical, then, that upgrades will be released, more apps and games will be developed, and at some point there will be a Fire TV 2.

We're going to indulge in just a bit of speculation on what a new and improved Fire TV would look like. Like all speculation, you win some and you lose some, but we're good with that.

First, we expect to see more channels in the near future. Users are clamoring for HBO Go and Walmart's Vudu video, and sports fans are asking for more sports channels, such as MLB.tv and NHL.tv.

Rest assured that negotiations are in progress, because that's how Amazon rolls.

Amazon has already promised that thousands more games and apps for the Fire TV will be available in the next year or two, and with their dedicated in-house development team on the job, they're positioned to keep that promise.

We're also hoping that screen mirroring will be available for more devices in addition to the Kindle Fire HDX. Mirroring for tablets, smartphones, and computers might be a bit much to ask, but it shouldn't be difficult to mirror from an Android tablet or phone to the Fire TV considering it runs on a modified Android operating system.

Bluetooth headphone capability for quiet listening shouldn't be a stretch either, considering the box is already Bluetooth enabled. Heck, we'll settle for a wired headphone jack!

Finally, we'd like to see Amazon open up the Fire TV's operating system more so that third-party developers can release apps for the device, just as Google has done with its Android smartphone.

The fact that the Android-based Fire TV doesn't accept third-party apps makes it plain that this was a deliberate decision on Amazon's part. Their spokespeople say it's for quality control, but the current lack of variety in the app department is a real down side. We hope they find a workable compromise on this in the near future.

COMING SOON: MORE DEVICES, MORE MEDIA FOR THE FIRE TV

Amazon is already promising Fire TV owners more goodies before the end of 2014. We're watching for their release and will update this section when they become available.

As we mentioned previously, Amazon is promising an update for the Fire TV that will add MP3 music streaming for any Amazon-purchased songs and albums stored in your Amazon Cloud account. This update won't include music you purchased from sellers other than Amazon, such as iTunes, but it's still a major step forward.

The update will even let you stream music you purchased from Amazon on CD. With Amazon's X-ray feature, you'll be able to view song lyrics while the music is playing, a feature that's already available for the Kindle.

Amazon will also add support for iOS to its Second Screen feature, allowing iPhone and iPad owners to "fling" the screen display on those devices to their Fire TV. This feature is already enabled on the Kindle Fire HDX. In addition to screen mirroring, Second Screen lets you view X-ray data, powered by IMDb, on your handheld device and use it as a remote while you watch the show on the Fire TV.

Amazon is also releasing a Fire TV app for smartphones and tablets that will extend remote functions and controls for touch-enabled games.

That's a lot to look forward to. In the meantime, we've found our Fire TV to be insane amounts of fun. We hope you enjoy it – we have!

A FINAL QUICK REMINDER ABOUT UPDATES

As we mentioned at the start of this book, the Amazon Fire TV and indeed all media streaming services, like Apple TV, Roku and the Chromecast, are still in their infancy. The landscape is changing all the time with new services, apps and media suppliers appearing daily.

Staying on top of new developments is our job and if you sign up to our free monthly newsletter we will keep you abreast of news, tips and tricks for all your streaming media equipment.

If you want to take advantage of this, sign up for the updates HERE…

www.Lyntons.com/updates

Don't worry; we hate spam as much as you do so we will never share your details with anyone.

37775038R00041

Made in the USA
Lexington, KY
13 December 2014